Praise for *ABCs of Crabbing on the C...*

"This beautifully written and illustrated book is perfect for anyone who loves the waters in and around the Chesapeake Bay. If you have a father, grandfather, husband, or son who makes their living as a waterman, it is the perfect story to pass on to future generations that will one day become a waterman or woman! Anyone who loves a hot steamed crab should share this ABC story of crabbing with little ones."

—Shauna Deihl McCranie
Executive Director,
Reedville Fishermen's Museum,
Daughter of a menhaden fish boat captain

"As a lifelong outdoorsman and steward of the Chesapeake Bay, I've experienced firsthand the joy that comes from being on the water. Susan Swift's *ABCs of Crabbing on the Chesapeake Bay* wonderfully details the work of watermen during the process of harvesting blue crabs and is a great read for those who want an easy, yet eye-catching, introduction to the industry."

—Congressman Rob Wittman (VA-01)

"What a perfect book for anyone who visits or lives near the Chesapeake Bay! As someone who grew up in a commercial fishing family, I appreciate that this story shares the process of what many Chesapeake Bay watermen do to harvest crabs. The story is written in language that is easy to understand, and the illustrations are simple yet beautiful. *The ABCs of Crabbing* highlights an important product of the Chesapeake Bay, and appeals to everyone, whether you are one or one hundred!"

—Lynn Haynie Kellum,
President of Ampro Shipyard and
Diesel, and Virginia Marine Resource
Commission (VMRC) Board Member

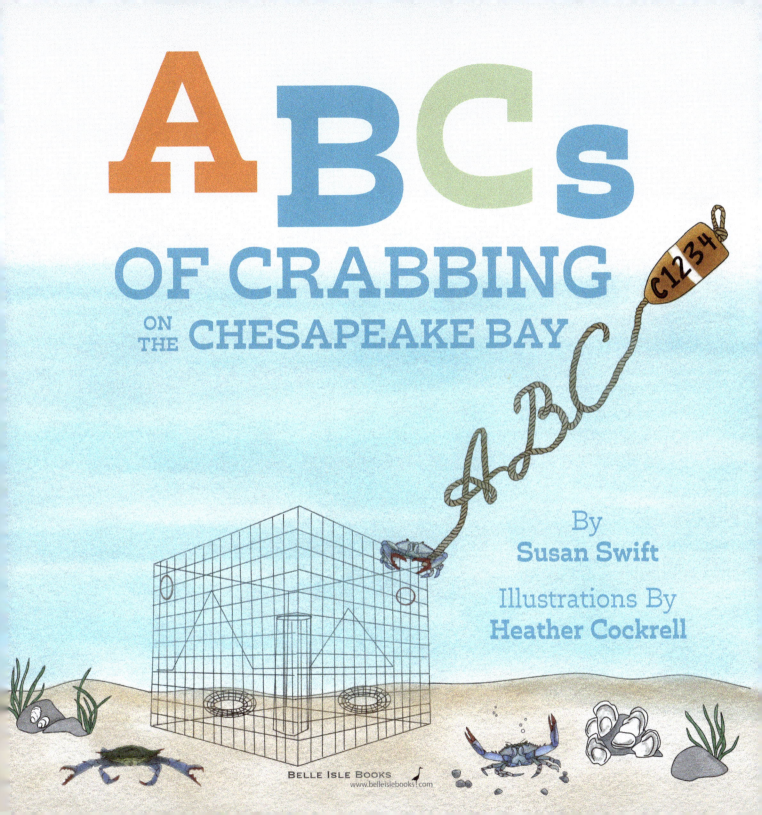

Copyright © 2024 by Susan Swift

No part of this book may be reproduced in any form or by any electronic or mechanical means, or the facilitation thereof, including information storage and retrieval systems, without permission in writing from the publisher, except in the case of brief quotations published in articles and reviews. Any educational institution wishing to photocopy part or all of the work for classroom use, or individual researchers who would like to obtain permission to reprint the work for educational purposes, should contact the publisher.

ISBN: 978-1-962416-38-2

Library of Congress Control Number: 2024909553

Designed by Sami Langston

Production managed by Maryanna Stufflebeem

Printed in the United States of America

Published by

Belle Isle Books (an imprint of Brandylane Publishers, Inc.)

5 S. 1st Street

Richmond, Virginia 23219

BELLE ISLE BOOKS
www.belleislebooks.com

belleislebooks.com | brandylanepublishers.com

For my two favorite watermen, Keith and Zach,
and to Macy, my cheerleader.

Foreword

Until I moved to the town of Reedville in the Northern Neck of Virginia — where the Potomac River meets the Chesapeake Bay — the only experience I had with crabs was ordering them in a restaurant! Then I met my husband, who is a fourth-generation waterman. He and my son crab during the year in the rivers in and around the Chesapeake Bay. I have learned that harvesting crabs is hard work! It is also pretty interesting. This book is dedicated to them.

I hope you will enjoy learning about what commercial watermen do in order for us to enjoy delicious crabs!

- S.S.

is for ABOARD

All *aboard*! In order to harvest crabs, watermen need to get on boats, because crabs live in and around the rivers and shores of the Chesapeake Bay. The bay is the perfect mix of fresh and salt water for them.

B is for BLUE CRAB

The Chesapeake Bay is famous for its blue crabs, which really do have a bluish-green color. They turn red when they are cooked.

Did you know crabs outgrow their shells? A peeler is a crab that is about to come out of its old shell in order to grow. Watermen separate the peelers from the hard crabs until they shed their old shell and their new shell hardens. Otherwise, they might get eaten by other crabs when they shed!

Chesapeake Bay

 **is for CHESAPEAKE BAY**

The Chesapeake Bay, on the east coast of the United States, is surrounded by the states of Virginia, Maryland, and Delaware. It is full of wildlife, including sea animals like blue crabs, as well as many types of fish and birds.

D is for DOCK

Watermen use a *dock*, or a wooden walkway over the water, to get into and out of their boats and to move crabs and supplies on and off the boat.

 **is for ESCAPE RING**

The *escape ring*, or cull ring, is a special hole on the side of the crab pot that allows the smallest crabs to swim back into the water where they can continue to grow. Crab pots in Virginia have two escape rings.

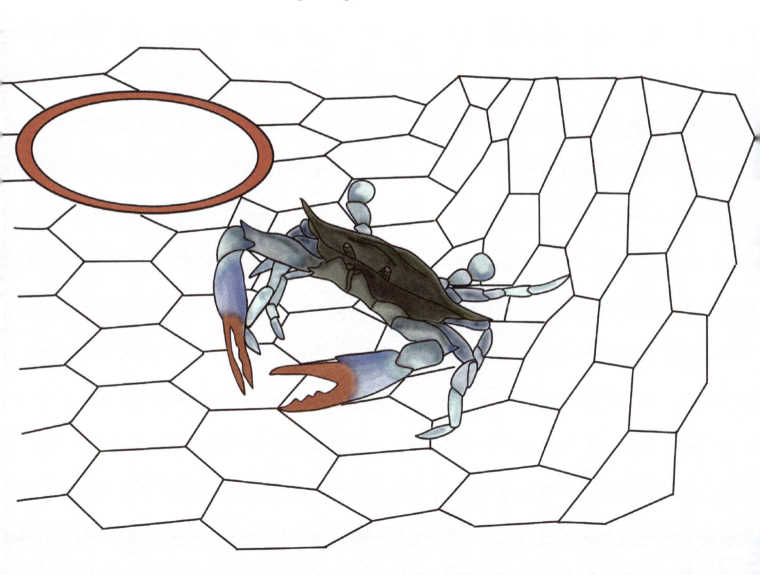

 **is for FIVE PAIRS OF LEGS**

Although crabs are known for their strong front claws, they actually have ten legs; *five on each side*. Their front claws help them grip or grab things, and the other eight legs help them move. Blue crabs can move forward but prefer to move sideways, because they move more quickly that way.

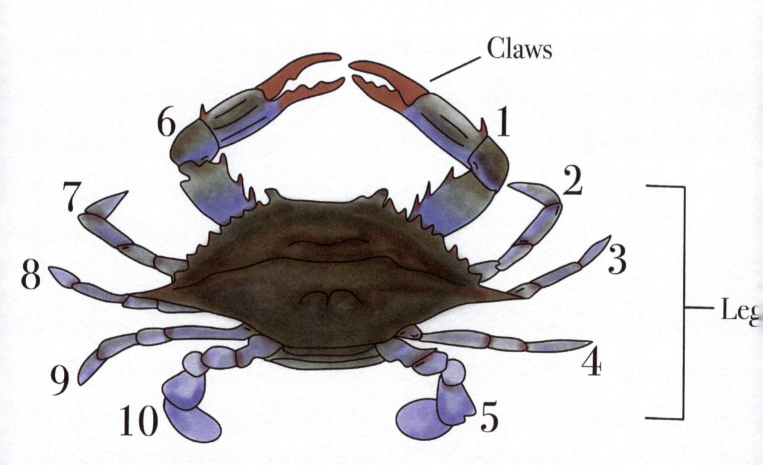

G is for GILLS

Like fish, crabs live underwater. They have gills, which filter oxygen from the water to help them breathe.

is for HALF HITCH KNOT

A *half hitch knot* is an important knot for watermen. They use these knots to secure a boat to a dock post, which keeps the boat in place when they reach the dock with their crabs.

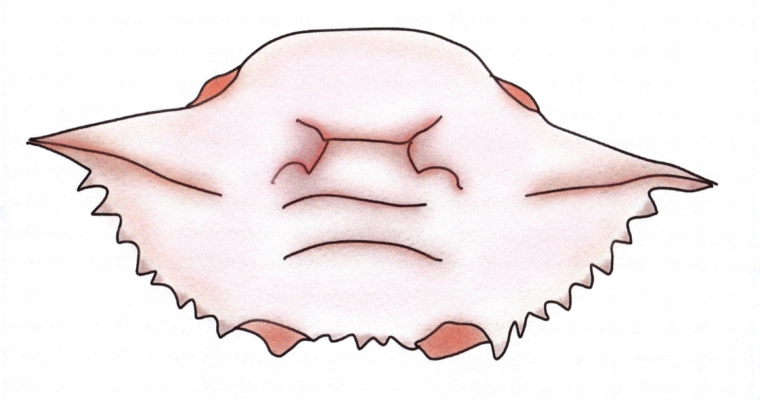

I is for INVERTEBRATE

Crabs do not have backbones like people do. They are called *invertebrates*. Their shells, or exoskeletons, protect their insides.

J is for JIMMY

Jimmy can be a boy's name, and it is also a name for a male crab. They grow bigger than female crabs. You can tell a male crab by turning him over. He has a shape that looks like the Washington monument on his belly.

is for KEEPER

A *keeper* is what watermen call crabs that are big enough to keep. In the Chesapeake Bay, crabs must be five inches from tip to tip in order to keep. This rule gives the smaller crabs time to grow and protects crabs from being overharvested.

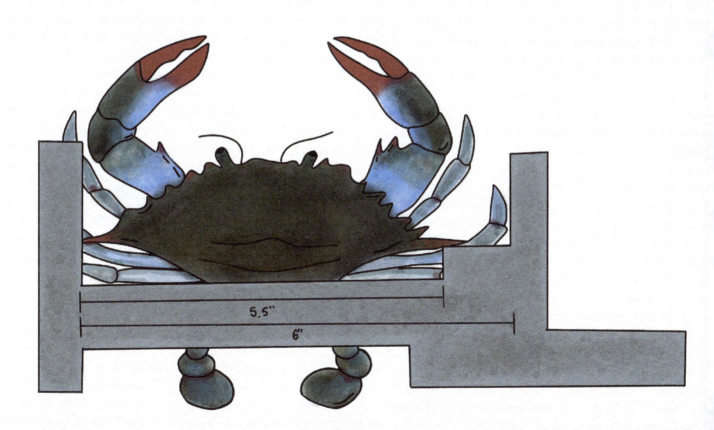

L is for LINE

Crab pots are put out, or "set," in *lines* in the water. Setting their pots in these rows helps watermen determine where the best crabbing areas are at the time. Watermen move lines often.

M is for MENHADEN

Menhaden are oily fish that people don't eat, but they are still very important. Other sea creatures eat them, but watermen use them as bait in crab pots. Watermen put menhaden inside of a "bait box" in the crab pot. The bait lures the crabs into the pot.

N is for NOCTURNAL

Did you know that crabs are *nocturnal*? They are most active at night. This protects them from predators, or animals who want to eat them.

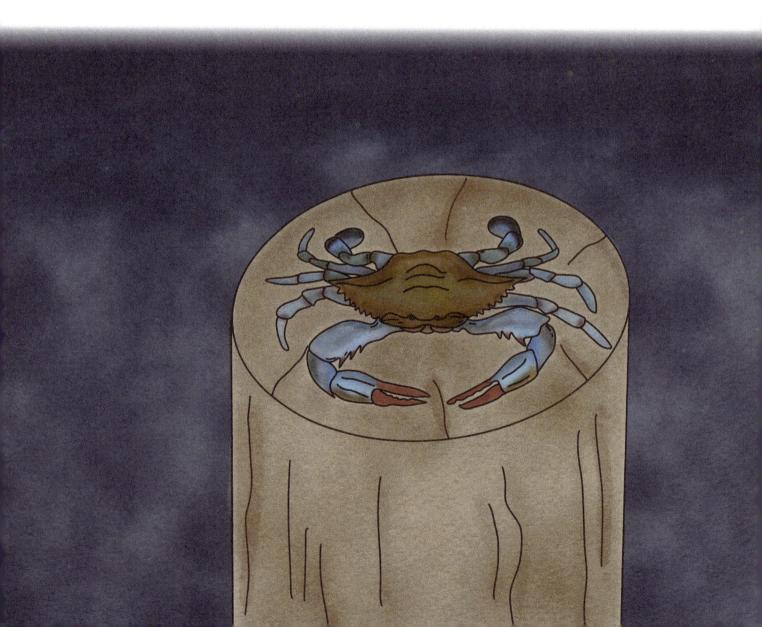

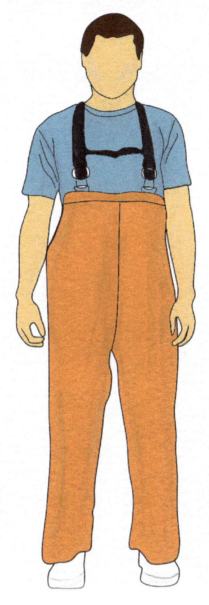

 **is for OILSKINS**

Oilskins are waterproof overalls that watermen wear. Oilskins keep watermen from getting wet while they harvest crabs. They are often bright yellow, white, or orange.

P is for POT PULLER

After a waterman catches his line and buoy with a long stick called a gaff, he hooks it around a motorized *pot puller*. The pot puller winds the line around it, pulling the crab pot up to the top of the water. The waterman pulls the pot in, shakes the pot, and empties the crabs onto a table, or cull box, to sort through and measure each one.

 **is for QUOTA**

A **quota** is the maximum number of crabs that can be caught. Every waterman must have a license that says how many crab pots they can have out at one time and how many bushels of crabs they can harvest each day. This ensures that crabs will be plentiful in the Chesapeake Bay for us to enjoy for many years to come.

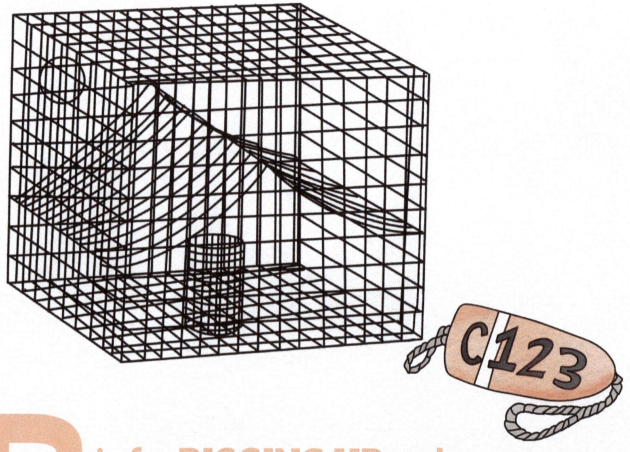

R is for RIGGING UP crab pots

Rigging up pots means getting crab pots ready to put into the water. Crab pots are made with wire mesh, made into the shape of a cube. Each crab pot has four funnels where the crabs crawl in, and one side that opens so that the crabs can be taken out. Once they crawl in, they cannot get out. Watermen paint the crab pots, add zincs to each pot, paint and number their buoys, and measure and attach the line and the buoys in order to get them ready to catch crabs.

S is for SOOK

A sook is the name for a female crab. Sooks are usually smaller than jimmys but their meat is equally as delicious! A sook has an apron on her belly that looks like a temple.

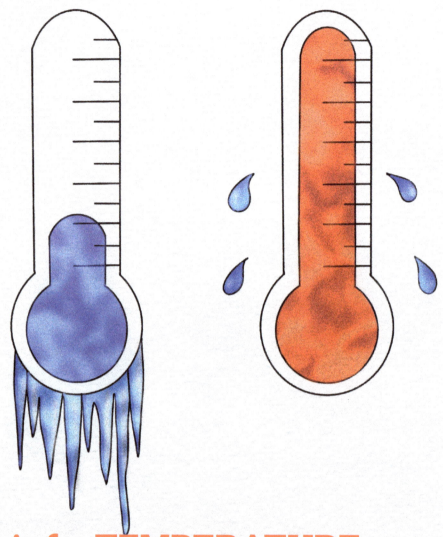

T is for TEMPERATURE

Water temperature affects crabs! Crabs are caught from the spring through the fall, when the water is warm and they are active. During the winter, when the water is cold, crabs burrow down into the mud.

 **is for UNDERWATER**

Because crabs live underwater, watermen must tie a buoy to each crab pot using a long line, and drop the pot into the water. The buoys float on the water, and help the watermen identify their own crab pots. Each waterman paints their buoys differently and puts their special crabbing license number on them. In Virginia, each float begins with the letter C and is followed by the waterman's identification number.

V is for VESSEL

A fishing *vessel* is a fancy name for a boat. Each vessel has a number displayed on the side, and owners usually name their boats. The names can be seen on the back or the side of the boat. Some watermen use a Chesapeake Bay deadrise boat to harvest crabs, and others use skiffs, which are both flat bottom boats that make it easy for the watermen to work.

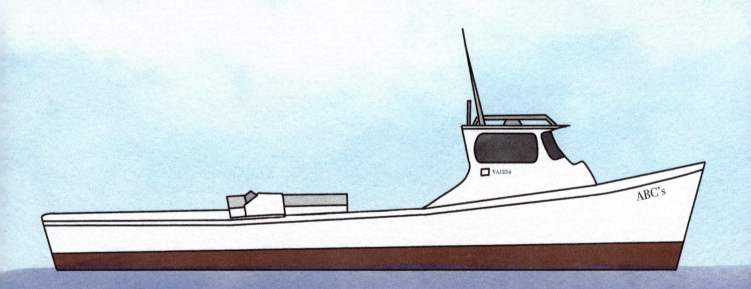

W is for WATERMAN

Watermen are the men and women who catch seafood like the crabs that we enjoy eating during the spring and summer!

 **is for eXtra Early in the Morning**

There are rules about when watermen can harvest crabs. During crab season, that time starts at sunrise, which is *eXtra early* in the morning! This means that watermen are up before sunrise in order to make sure they have gas in the boat, bait for their crab pots, and all of the bushel baskets they need on the boat to hold their catch!

 **is for YUMMY!**

Many people think that crab meat tastes yummy! In the Chesapeake Bay region, people like to steam crabs and serve them with butter, vinegar, Old Bay seasoning, or cocktail sauce. They spread newspaper onto the table, put a pile of the cooked crabs in the middle, and everyone "picks" their crabs, or takes them apart, eating the meat.

is for ZINC

Zincs are special pieces of metal that watermen put onto crab pots to keep them from rusting or corroding. Putting zincs on the crab pots helps them last longer underwater.

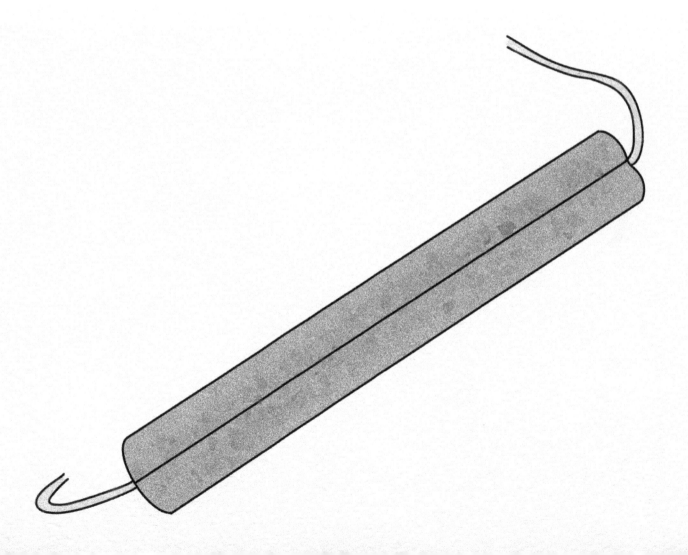

About the Author

Susan Swift obtained her B.A. and M.A.Ed. at The College of William and Mary. She has been an elementary teacher, a reading specialist, and a librarian for many years. An avid reader, she has wanted to write children's books since she first became a teacher. She was inspired to write this book because she moved from Pennsylvania to the Northern Neck of Virginia after college, and did not know the first thing about crabbing, or how any kinds of seafood were harvested. She lives on the Chesapeake Bay and wanted to highlight the work of local watermen, like her husband, son, and friends, working on the Chesapeake Bay.

She has two grown children, and lives in Reedville, Virginia, with her husband and two very spoiled dogs. She enjoys spending time with her family, going to the beach, reading, and writing.

About the Illustrator

Heather Cockrell has always had a passion for using her creativity to inspire children to express their own unique creativity. Heather was born and raised in the small rural town of Lancaster County, Virginia. After graduating from high school, Heather attended Ferrum College, where she received her bachelor's degree in Education. After teaching for a few years in several different areas in Virginia, Heather decided to return home and accepted her current position as the middle school art teacher at Northumberland Middle School in Northumberland County, Virginia. Heather now resides in the small town of Reedville, Virginia with her husband Nick and their two dogs. She enjoys spending time on the water that both she and her husband grew up on.

Printed in the USA
CPSIA information can be obtained
at www.ICGtesting.com
CBHW060244130724
11509CB00034B/1006